Let's Talk About
Children
Around the World

Debby Anderson

The Sunwar
Himalayas

"Hello!"
India

Paraguay

Chariot Books™
A Division of Cook Communications, Inc.

Russia

Andile Holiday
South Africa

Yung Mee Park
Korea

Bulan Pupardtong
Thailand

The children our family has enjoyed sponsoring

Dear Family and Friends,

Children are a most precious treasure. The possibilities that God has hidden in each one are astounding. But most children around the world lack the resources to develop these possibilities. Education, health care, family security, and safety are only a dream.

Consider an opportunity to help a child's dream come true. Through sponsorship programs, you can share God's love and care with a treasured child, a child whose name, photos, and letters will become treasures of your own. Consider the possibilities!

D. A.

Chariot Books™ is an imprint of David C. Cook Publishing Co.
David C. Cook Publishing Co., Elgin, Illinois 60120
David C. Cook Publishing Co., Weston, Ontario
Nova Distribution Ltd., Eastbourne, England

LET'S TALK ABOUT CHILDREN AROUND THE WORLD
©1994 by Debby Anderson for text and illustrations.

Designed by Donna Nelson

Printed in the United States of America

ISBN 0-7814-0178-X

Sponsorships available through:
COMPASSION   1 800 336-7676
WORLD VISION 1 800 423-4200

Gratefully acknowledging:
Dr. Walt Baker and Dr. Robert J. Choun,
        Dallas Theological Seminary
Linda Leonard,
        International Students, Inc.
Our World
        National Geographic Society
National Geographic
        National Geographic Society
Target Earth
        Global Mapping International

For more information on cross-cultural ministries in the United States, call:
        American Missionary Fellowship
        1 215 527-4439

Hawaii
U.S.A.

Samoa

Dedicated with love to my grandparents:
    Catherine Duffy Purcell, 1895-1973
    Walter Evans Purcell, 1887-1973
    Missionaries to Canada, India, and
    the U. S.A.

Come on! . . .

Peru   Australia   Poland   Burkina Faso

. . . let's play!

All around the world,
children have fun playing.
God made us that way!
We love to run and jump
and climb and laugh.

India

Israel

The Gypsies
Romania

Korea

Spain

Ropes twirl on every
continent except
Antarctica . . . unless
penguins can jump!

Zaire   U.S.A.

El Salvador

Cuba

Albania

Denmark

Bahamas   Irian Jaya

Dominican Republic

Ecuador

Brazil

Madagascar

Germany

The Napu Indonesia

Sergio is leading his friends in a game of pega-pega (tag).

Uruguay

Belize

Armenia

Kuwait

U.S.A.

Children everywhere study and learn and explore.

1 2 3 4 5 6 7 8 9 10 11 12 13 14 15 16 17 18 19 20 21 22 23 24 25 26 27 28 29 30 31 32 33 34 35 36 37 38 39 40 41 42

The Sikhs
Canada

England

Russia

On "Teacher's Day,"
Tanya thanks her
teacher with flowers

Jesus
Loves
Me

The Bible teaches us
about God's love!

Sri Lanka

U.S.A.

Mongolia

Japan

Kazumi and her
friends wear
uniforms.

Australia

43 44 45 46 47 48 49 50 51 52 53

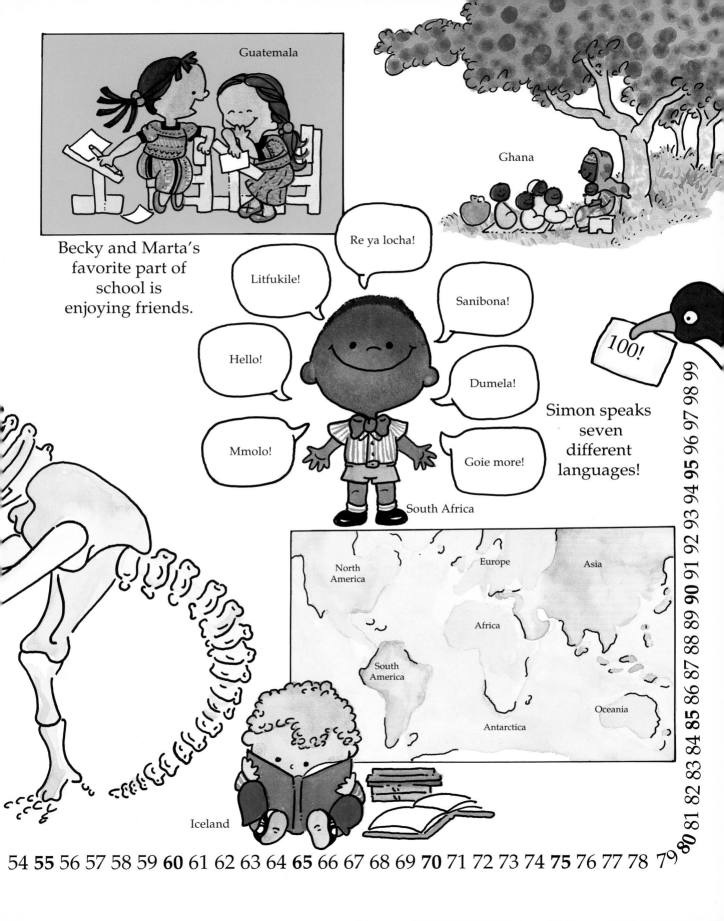

Guatemala

Becky and Marta's
favorite part of
school is
enjoying friends.

Ghana

Re ya locha!

Litfukile!

Sanibona!

Hello!

Dumela!

Mmolo!

Goie more!

Simon speaks
seven
different
languages!

South Africa

100!

North
America

Europe

Asia

Africa

South
America

Oceania

Antarctica

Iceland

54 **55** 56 57 58 59 **60** 61 62 63 64 **65** 66 67 68 69 **70** 71 72 73 74 **75** 76 77 78 79 **80** 81 82 83 84 **85** 86 87 88 89 **90** 91 92 93 94 **95** 96 97 98 99

All around the world children help their moms and dads with chores.

Austria

The Plain People U.S.A.

Mali

Papua New Guinea

Ethiopia

Argentina

Vietnam

Yemen

Uganda

The Kurds/Iraq

Belgium

Brazil

Mexico

Pakistan

China

Lok Si knows the most important job
of all is caring for younger children!

Great
Britain

El Salvador

Peru

Newfoundland
Canada

Morocco

Ghana

U.S.A.

Greece

Somalia

SEWING
KNITTING

Oops!

Kenya

Austria

Haiti

THE
HIGHLAND
FLING
Scotland

GUITAR
Bolivia

Children everywhere perform, make
music, and create amazing works of art.

MODELS
Macau

COPPER
TOOLING
Lebanon

BRASS BAND
Honduras

CARVING

DRAWING
Bhutan

Burkina
Faso

The Maori
New Zealand

CHINESE OPERA
Taiwan

Sierra Leone

Chad

PUPPETS
Mexico

BALAFON
Cote d'lvoire

Tamba and Pascal can make cars and trucks out of anything, just as other boys all over Africa do.

VEGGIE SCULPTURES
Israel

Japan

POPCORN
RING DANCE
The Napu
Indonesia

The Philippines

Papua New Guinea

Together, Mona and Sofi are weaving a new sleeping mat.

PAPER
CUTTING
China

All around the world children play games and sports together.

KARATE
Japan

Romania

Skiing is Miles's favorite.

Canada

Korea

Finland

SKATING   TOBOGGANING

BADMINTON

Macau

Austria

Zaire

Paraguay

Sweden

Vietnam

Mexico

MARBLES

Katie is trying to win a new blue glassie!

GYMNASTICS
Taiwan

The Maranao
The Philippines

CHESS   Latvia

Malaysia

ARCHERY
Kalahari Desert

Soccer is everywhere!

Cambodia   Ireland

Pani gets a ride and a bath at the same time!

ELEPHANTS
Thailand

United Arab Emirates
FALCONS

CAMELS
The Ribari
India

SHEEP

Wales

The Navajo
U.S.A.

Ireland
COW

WATER BUFFALO
Laos

We take care of different pets and animals.

The Palestinians
Israel

TURTLE
Colombia

Czechoslovakia

Dogs and cats are everywhere!

OSTRICH
Texas, U.S.A.

GOATS
The Afar Nomads
Djibouti

Australia

Rachel gives "Willy," her 6-foot pet kangaroo, a hug.

Costa Rica

Because the places we live are so different, we build different kinds of houses and wear different kinds of clothes.

Tibet

Macau

The Mangyan
The Philippines

Zaire

Russia

Curacao Island
The Caribbean

Chile

Raisha's home can move from place to place, just like the wind.

The Sahara

China

Taiwan

The Ndebele
South Africa

On Easter Monday in Poland, boys and girls have "smigus dyngus"— water fights!

Nader is watching fireworks flash over Egypt's Nile River. All around the world, fireworks are part of New Year's, Christmas, Independence Day, and other celebrations.

We celebrate different holidays or the same holidays in different ways.

El Salvador's Christmas Posada Parade acts out Mary and Joseph's search for shelter. Tamales and foamy cocoa are the treats to eat.

Jay flies his kite in China's Kite Flying Festival.

In Greenland, Alice flies her kite just for fun!

Colored lights decorate the home during a Pakistani wedding.

Ahmad flies his kite in a Malaysian competition.

As a festival dance, "moko-jumbie" (stilt dancing) has traveled across the oceans from Africa to the Virgin Islands to Brooklyn, New York.

The end of Iran's New Year and Welcome Spring celebration includes a picnic with clowns, wrestlers, and tightrope walkers.

Mali

U.S.A.

China   Venezuela

Some collect baseball cards . . .
some collect stamps!

Australia

Argentina

Kenya

Angry   Happy   Scared   Confident

Caring

Singing

Cooking

Because God loves us, we can love each other. God has given every one of us different gifts and talents. Now and as you grow up, God wants you to use your gifts and talents to help others.

Helping

Building

Healing

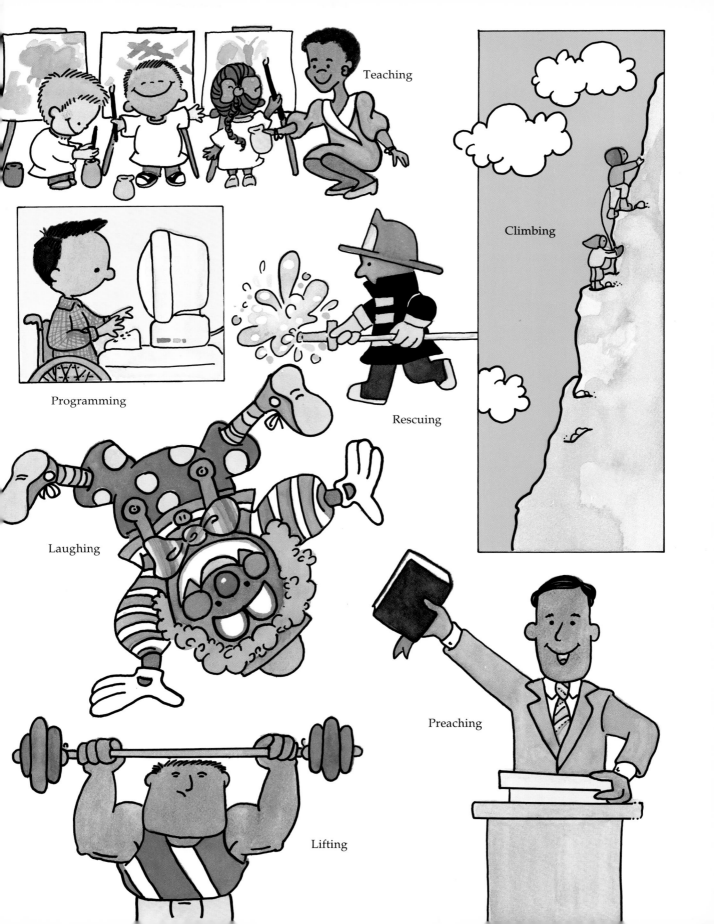

Teaching

Climbing

Programming

Rescuing

Laughing

Preaching

Lifting

Someday you might travel around the world . . . but right now, children from around the world might be living in your own neighborhood or going to your school.

Jamaica

Niger

" . . . You shine like stars in the universe as you hold out the word of life . . ."
Philippians 2:15, 16

Oman

Germany

Korea

Estonia

Ecuador

You can have fun learning new names and becoming friends. You can share each other's toys, smiles, and parties. You can even share the good news of Jesus' love.

Holland

Nigeria

Party 12:00

Wear Costumes

The Hmong U.S.A.

France

Around the

AUSTRALIA   Graham and Rachel Kell, Dallas Theological Seminary
AUSTRIA   Leslie Walt
BRAZIL   Lucia Okamoto Efferding, American Missionary Fellowship
BURKINA FASO   Laura Brinkerhoff, Wycliffe Bible Translators
CHINA   Yaoli Li, M. D.
                 Jay Shen
CURACAO ISLAND   Fernando Busby, American Missionary Fellowship
EL SALVADOR   Dr. Oscar Campos, Dallas Theological Seminary
GUATEMALA   Lilane Morales
HONG KONG   Carmen Tsui
INDIA   John Silvester Chikkala
                 Ammukutty George
IRIAN JAYA   Dave and Eleanor Bruce, UFM International
ISRAEL   Asma Albedd
JAPAN   Minori Ebihara
                 Takako Fukuda
KENYA   Dr. Roger and Shirley Brown, AIM
                 Jane Muthoni Munala, Dallas Theological Seminary
                 Paul Kinyanjui
KOREA   Hannah Hwa Sook Kim
MACAU   Audrey Fetters, Church of the United Brethren in Christ
MALAYSIA   Dr. M. Geevarughese, Pearly George
MEXICO   Esther Brambila, American Missionary Fellowship
                 Esther Santander, Sergio "Checho," Daniel
NIGERIA   Lillian Ogohi, Dallas Theological Seminary
                 Cindy Crutsinger, International Institute for Christian Studies
PAKISTAN   Mahjabeen Siddiqui
PAPUA NEW GUINEA Robin Rempel, Wycliffe Bible Translators
PARAGUAY   Rachel Kerr, American Missionary Fellowship
PERU   Ana Maria Campos, Becky
                 Dr. Stan and Sharon Pense, Christian Missions in Many Lands
PHILIPPINES   Bill and Yee-Fun Olsen, International Missions, Inc.
RUSSIA   Tatyana Chmykhalov
SIERRA LEONE   Tamba Bockarie
SOUTH AFRICA   Rev. Jerome and Mavis Nkosi, Urban Action
SPAIN   Rachel del Aguila Kull, Wycliffe Bible Translators
TAIWAN   Jei-Yin Fang
                 Liang-Tsu Hsieh
                 Gary and Kathy Webster, The Navigators
UNITED ARAB EMIRATES Scott and Carol Anderson, TEAM
UNITED STATES   Carrie Turansky, Josh, and Melissa (Hawaii)
                 Cynthia Nevels, Head Start of Greater Dallas
VIETNAM   Ngoc and Xuan-Dao Nguyen, Dallas Theological Seminary
                 Phong Cao
ZAIRE   Donna MacLean, CB International
                 Jane Winterling, Christian Missions in Many Lands

"Shukria!"
Pakistan

A BIG THANKS

• • • • • • • • •

to all who answered questions about their countries!

"Tenk yu!"
Irian Jaya

"Grazie!"
Italy

"Asante!"
Kenya

"Xie-Xie!"
China

"Sayonara!"
Japan

Nicaragua

The Wayana
French Guiana

The Kumas
Panama